Celebrating
**Hispanic
Diversity**

THE PEOPLE
AND CULTURE OF
PUERTO
RICO

Elizabeth Krajnik

PowerKiDS
press™

New York

Published in 2018 by The Rosen Publishing Group, Inc.
29 East 21st Street, New York, NY 10010

First Edition

Editor: Theresa Morlock
Book Design: Rachel Rising

Photo Credits:Cover, p. 25 Hola Images/Getty Images; Cover (background) Hamid Khan/EyeEm/ Getty Images; Cover, p. 1 https://commons.wikimedia.org/wiki/File:Flag_of_Puerto_Rico.svg; p. 4 ESB Professional/Shutterstock.com; p. 5 mikolajn/Shutterstock.com; p. 7 Gary Ives/Shutterstock.com; p. 9 CIS/ Shutterstock.com; p. 11 jcarillet/E+/Getty Images; p. 12 Bettmann/Contributor/Bettmann/Getty Images; p. 13 https://commons.wikimedia.org/wiki/File:Sonia_Sotomayor_in_SCOTUS_robe.jpg; p. 15 Wolfgang Kaehler/Contributor/LightRocket/Getty Images; p. 17 Rachel Moon/Shutterstock.com; p.19 Art Collection 4/Alamy Stock Photo; p. 21 Stephanie Maze/Corbis Documentary/Getty Images; p. 23 George Rose/Contributor/Getty Images News; p. 27 Jayne Kamin-Oncea/Stringer/Getty Images Sport/Getty Images; p. 29 Orlando/Stringer/Hulton Archive/Getty Images; p. 30 Brothers Good/ Shutterstock.com.

Library of Congress Cataloging-in-Publication Data

Names: Krajnik, Elizabeth, author.
Title: The people and culture of Puerto Rico / Elizabeth Krajnik.
Description: New York : PowerKids Press, 2018. | Series: Celebrating Hispanic diversity | Includes index.
Identifiers: LCCN 2017026249| ISBN 9781508163091 (library bound) | ISBN 9781538327050 (pbk.) | ISBN 9781538327494 (6 pack)
Subjects: LCSH: Puerto Rico–Juvenile literature.
Classification: LCC F1958.3 .K73 2018 | DDC 972.95–dc23
LC record available at https://lccn.loc.gov/2017026249

Manufactured in the United States of America

CPSIA Compliance Information: Batch #BW18PK: For Further Information contact Rosen Publishing, New York, New York at 1-800-237-9932

CONTENTS

GOING ON AN ADVENTURE

You're taking a trip to Puerto Rico, a beautiful island east of the Dominican Republic in the Caribbean Sea. But before you can pack your bags and board the plane, you must prepare yourself. What clothes should you bring? Do you need to learn a few Spanish phrases? What are the people like? To learn everything there is to know about Puerto Rico and its people would take a long time. This book will help you learn some important information about Puerto Rico's traditions, food, literature, and much more.

SAN JUAN

4

OLD SAN JUAN

San Juan is Puerto Rico's capital city. There, you can take a trip back in time by walking the cobbled streets and viewing the colonial architecture.

Puerto Rico is near the tropics. This means that the weather is warm and humid. The average high temperature throughout the year stays around 85º Fahrenheit (29.4º Celsius). Be sure to pack shorts and T-shirts!

COLUMBUS LANDS ON THE ISLAND

In 1493, the explorer Christopher Columbus landed on the island known today as Puerto Rico. However, this wasn't always the island's name. Columbus originally named the island San Juan Bautista, or Saint John the Baptist. After gold was discovered in a river, the island's name was changed to Puerto Rico, which means "rich port" in Spanish.

Puerto Rico wasn't uninhabited when Columbus arrived. A group of about 70,000 to 100,000 **indigenous** people, called the Taínos, lived on the island. The Taíno people had their own name for the island: Borikén, which means "the great land of the **valiant** and noble lord" in their language. Columbus conquered the island and made it an important Spanish colony, producing cattle and crops such as sugar cane and tobacco.

Puerto Rico was a very important colony. The Spanish built huge forts such as the Castillo de San Felipe del Morro (pictured here) to protect it from being conquered by other countries.

FIGHTING FOR INDEPENDENCE

Puerto Rico remained a part of the Spanish empire for around 400 years. However, this doesn't mean that the islanders were happy with their **circumstances**. Political unrest was frequent in the colony. In 1865, local officials requested that slavery be abolished. Many Spanish politicians took this to be the start of a **rebellion**. They arrested and sent some of the islanders to Spain for trial. This caused an uprising known as the Grito de Lares, or "Cry of Lares," on September 23, 1868.

In 1898, at the end of the Spanish-American War, Spain ceded, or gave up, Cuba, Puerto Rico, the Philippines, and Guam to the United States under the Treaty of Paris. This agreement prevented Puerto Ricans from establishing their own independent government. Puerto Rico then became a territory of the United States. In 1917, Puerto Ricans received U.S. citizenship.

When the United States gained control of Puerto Rico, it used the island as a port to load warships with coal. Puerto Rico served as a midway point between the United States and the Panama Canal.

The Fight Continues

In 1952, Puerto Rico became a U.S. commonwealth. That means it has its own constitution and government but is also subject to the U.S. government. Some Puerto Rican people wish for U.S. statehood. In June 2016, Puerto Rico's governor, Alejandro J. García Padilla, spoke to the United Nations in New York City about Puerto Rico's status as an associated free state. This means that Puerto Rico is self-governing but the United States controls its trade, military, and more. Puerto Ricans are divided on the issue of statehood. Many continue to fight for complete independence.

Today, most Puerto Ricans practice Catholicism. When the Spanish arrived on the island, they brought their religion with them. Their beliefs mixed with those of the Taínos and Africans—who were the Spaniards' slaves. A new religion, which is referred to as Espiritismo, or spiritualism, was created. The followers of Espiritismo believe in magical forces that can be good or bad.

Espiritismo is still practiced today. It is common for Puerto Rican families to place bowls of fruit in their kitchens to keep away vampire-like creatures. Similarly, parents often give their children charms to protect them from the "evil eye," which is when a person becomes sick from being jealous of someone else's belongings.

Catholicism is the most popular religion in Puerto Rico. The figure of Christ pictured here stands in the **Cathedral** of San Juan Bautista, which was built in 1521 and is one of the oldest structures in the country.

11

NOTABLE PUERTO RICANS

One of Puerto Rico's most notable historic heroes is Pedro Albizu Campos. Campos was the leader of the Puerto Rican **Nationalist** Party. He and other members of the party fought for Puerto Rico's independence in the mid-20th century. Campos was in and out of U.S. prisons for 25 years because of his involvement with the Nationalist Party.

Today, many Puerto Ricans consider Campos the father of the Puerto Rican independence movement. Even after being imprisoned, he resumed fighting for his country's right to rule itself.

SONIA SOTOMAYOR

Sonia Sotomayor became the first Latina and person of Puerto Rican descent to hold the position of associate justice of the U.S. Supreme Court. President Barack Obama nominated her for the position on May 26, 2009. Sotomayor was born in the Bronx, a part of New York City, and has Puerto Rican heritage. She had a very large role in upholding part of the Affordable Care Act, or Obamacare, in a court ruling in 2015.

REASON TO CELEBRATE

Holidays are an important part of every culture. Even though Puerto Rico is part of the United States, it has its own special holidays and celebrations. Like other countries with Spanish influence, Puerto Rico celebrates El Día de los Tres Reyes Magos, or Three Kings Day, on January 6. In many Hispanic countries, this day is often more important than Christmas!

The week before Ash Wednesday is a time of serious celebrating. In the city of Ponce, there is a celebration that is like Puerto Rico's own Mardi Gras. The Ponce Carnival dates to the 1700s, and it's the most celebrated festival in Puerto Rico. Characters called *vejigantes* walk around the festival wearing monster masks. The festival ends with a comical ceremony called El Entierro de la Sardina, or the Burial of the Sardine.

The people in this photo are wearing *vejigante* costumes at a festival in Ponce, Puerto Rico.

Who Are the *Vejigantes?*

The *vejigantes* are demons from Puerto Rican **folklore**, which has its roots in African, Spanish, and Caribbean culture. They get their name from the word *vejiga*, which means "bladder" in Spanish. The *vejigantes* walk around the carnival with inflated cow bladders, which they use to beat evil spirits out of children and other carnival goers. El Entierro de la Sardina marks the coming season of Lent. The coffin and dummy sardine are lit on fire, symbolizing the burning away of the sins of the flesh.

TASTY TREATS

Puerto Rican food is very special. All the cultures of people who have settled on the island—Taíno, Spanish, Cuban, African, American, and more—influence Puerto Rican food. This cuisine is a lot like Creole food from Louisiana. Puerto Ricans call their traditional dishes *cocina criolla*, or Creole cooking. This type of food features ingredients and spices that are native to the island, such as coriander, papaya, and cacao.

One of Puerto Rico's most classic dishes is *asopao*, which is a thick soup similar to gumbo. Each person has a different way of preparing *asopao*, but most recipes have chicken or shellfish. Stews are a popular main dish in Puerto Rico and can be made with many different ingredients. Coconut is one of the most common ingredients in Puerto Rican desserts.

Mofongo, shown here, is a popular Puerto Rican dish. It's made with plantains that are fried and mashed. it can be mixed with different vegetables and meats.

FABULOUS FINE ARTS

Many Puerto Ricans have become famous for their art, singing, writing, and acting. Art is a very important part of Puerto Rican life, and many talented artists have drawn inspiration from their beautiful island. The Museo de Arte de Ponce is the greatest art museum in Puerto Rico.

Puerto Rican literature started around the time when Spanish explorers began to colonize the island. However, this literature was often written by the settlers and not the inhabitants of the island. One of the most important Puerto Rican writers is the poet Julia de Burgos.

After many years of U.S. political control, many Puerto Rican authors, such as Alejandro Tapía y Rivera, who is considered the father of Puerto Rican literature, began publishing written works about their experiences as people who weren't official U.S. citizens.

José Campeche, pictured here, is perhaps one of the first Puerto Rican artists to achieve fame. His work was created with San Juan as his muse. He also painted events from the Bible.

PUERTO RICAN FOLKLORE

Puerto Rican culture is a mixture of Taíno, Spanish, and African influences. Each of these cultures contributed elements of its folklore to Puerto Rican folklore.

When the Spanish first arrived on the island, they recorded the stories that the Taíno people told most often. These stories often featured creatures that would walk around at night in search of food or people. Some tales also referenced nature getting even with humans. This revenge could take the form of hurricanes.

A popular figure in Puerto Rican folklore is *el jíbaro*. This name is taken from a Puerto Rican word that means "country." The figure of *el jíbaro* is from the country or mountains and often featured in Puerto Rican literature and art. Puerto Ricans use this word both affectionately and to insult people.

Musician Carmelo Martel Luciano is pictured here playing a cuatro. The cuatro has the seven districts of Puerto Rico painted on it.

Folk Music and Art

Music and art play an important role in preserving Puerto Rican folk traditions. Carmelo Martel Luciano, pictured above, is well known for his contributions to folk culture. He made and played an instrument called the cuatro, which is the national instrument of Puerto Rico. His beautifully crafted cuatros are considered masterpieces of folk art and are on display in the Museo de la Música Puertorriqueña (Puerto Rican Music Museum) in Ponce.

WHAT DO PUERTO RICANS WEAR?

Even though Puerto Rico is a part of the United States, the island still has its own culture and traditional clothing. On an ordinary day, you will probably see people wearing clothes identical to those worn by people in the mainland United States. However, on certain occasions, Puerto Ricans wear special clothing rich with their island's history.

The guayabera is a type of men's shirt. These shirts are fitted to each person. They have pockets on the front, aren't too tight, and are worn with dress pants. Traditional guayaberas, which are usually worn on formal occasions, are made from fibers from the pineapple plant.

Historically, the Taíno people wore very little clothing. Only married women wore clothes, which were skirts called *naguas*. Men and women decorated their bodies with paint and jewelry.

At a quinceañera, the young girl will dance with her father. Then she'll dance with the boy who escorted her. This is the most anticipated part of the party.

Quinceañeras

Young girls in Puerto Rico have a party called a quinceañera to celebrate their 15th birthday. They wear big gowns that look similar to wedding gowns or prom dresses. A girl's quinceañera marks her **transition** from childhood into adulthood. Because Aztec and Mayan cultures also had celebrations to mark the transition from childhood to adulthood, it's believed that the quinceañera may have partly been inspired by Aztec and Mayan traditions. Quinceañeras begin with a religious ceremony, and afterward there is a big party.

Music is a very important part of many cultures around the world. Puerto Rico's rich history features some interesting musical traditions. The guiro is a gourd that has been hollowed out and has ridges with which to make sounds. This instrument is used in traditional music and originates from the Taíno people.

Two types of popular music for dancing are bomba and *plena*. Bomba is created when drummers use their hands to strike tightly stretched animal skins. There are also rhythm sticks and maracas. This type of music originated in Africa.

Plena has its roots in Puerto Rico's many different cultural influences. It is created when the guiro, the cuatro, and the tambourine-like *pandero* are played together. People dance and talk about the events of the day, almost like a play or musical.

Traditional dances, such as salsa, are an important part of Puerto Rican culture. The music that goes along with salsa dancing, also called salsa, likely originated in New York City after World War II.

25

Before the Spanish arrived in Puerto Rico, the Taíno people had their own sports. Some of these were played as part of ceremonies, while others were played for fun. They had races, held fishing competitions, and tested each other's strength.

Playing sports and watching sporting events have become an important part of Puerto Rican culture. Today, Puerto Rico's sports attract many tourists from around the world. People from the United States and other cultures also enjoy most of the sports played in Puerto Rico. Some of the most popular sports played on the island include baseball, basketball, boxing, and soccer. Some consider baseball to be the most popular sport. In 1897, the first two baseball clubs were established after a group of Puerto Ricans visited the United States.

Puerto Rico's baseball teams participate in the Caribbean World Series. Many Puerto Ricans have become Major League Baseball players.

Batu

The Taínos played a game called *batu*, which closely resembles Roman gladiator fighting. *Batu* matches were held on U-shaped fields, called *batey*, which were also used as meeting places and ceremonial grounds. The games played there involved using the body to keep a ball moving. Two teams made up of people from different communities came together to fight. The winners of this difficult game were treated very well. However, the losers were sacrificed. When the Spanish arrived, they prevented the Taínos from playing *batu*.

27

MOVING TO THE UNITED STATES

For many years, Puerto Ricans have moved from the island to the mainland United States. This **migration** was especially large after World War II ended. Most people went to New York City. In 1910, fewer than 2,000 Puerto Ricans were living in the city. In 1945, there were about 13,000. In 1946, there were more than 50,000. These numbers increased each year, with a peak in 1953. Why did so many Puerto Ricans leave their homeland?

The war years were hard on everyone, but they were especially hard for Puerto Ricans. The island was experiencing an economic depression, and moving to the United States gave people a second chance at living a comfortable life. This was coupled with U.S. factory owners looking for workers. At that time, air travel was more affordable than ever.

Many Puerto Ricans lived in the poorest parts of New York City. Northeastern Manhattan became known as Spanish Harlem due to the large population of Puerto Ricans who settled there.

Today, Puerto Rico's vibrant culture can be seen on the island and throughout the United States. Even though many Puerto Ricans have established communities in the United States, their traditions have roots in their homeland. A large number of Puerto Ricans moved to the United States during the mid-20th century. Today's generations of Puerto Rican Americans continue to contribute to American society.

Many Puerto Ricans have worked hard to overcome prejudice against them. In 1992, Nydia Velázquez became the first Puerto Rican woman to be elected to the U.S. Congress. Poets and artists have fought for their voice in America at the Nuyorican Poets Cafe in New York City for more than 50 years.

Puerto Rican culture is rich with history, talent, and intelligence. Every year, Puerto Ricans bring their skills to America and further their cultural impact on the world.

GLOSSARY

architecture: A style of building.

cathedral: A large church that is the official seat of a bishop.

circumstance: A condition at a certain time or place.

cobbled: Paved or covered with cobblestones, or round stones often used in paving streets.

folklore: Ideas or stories that may not be true but that many people have heard or read.

indigenous: Living naturally in a particular region.

migration: Movement from one place to another.

muse: A source of inspiration.

nationalist: Relating to a political group that wants to form a separate and independent nation.

rebellion: Open fighting against authority or a fight to overthrow a government.

transition: A passage from one state, stage, or place to another.

valiant: Boldly brave or done with courage.

INDEX

WEBSITES

Due to the changing nature of Internet links, PowerKids Press has developed an online list of
websites related to the subject of this book. This site is updated regularly. Please use this link to
access the list: www.powerkidslinks.com/chd/puerto